SPORTS MOVIE P(

volume four of
the illustrated history of movies throug

Compiled by Richard Allen and Bruce Hershenson

Published by BRUCE HERSHENSON
P.O. Box 874, West Plains, MO 65775
(417) 256-9616 (phone) • (417) 256-0686 (fax)

TABLE OF CONTENTS

INTRODUCTION

Welcome to the fourth volume of **The Illustrated History of Movies Through Posters**. Volume One in the series is **Cartoon Movie Posters**, Volume Two is **Cowboy Movie Posters** and Volume Three is **Academy Award® Winners' Movie Posters**.

This book is an overview of the more than one thousand films that have been made about dozens of sports, both amateur and professional. The films that were included were chosen from four categories: films that have a sports theme, memorable films that have a major scene involving a sport, films that have poster art depicting a sport, and films that don't concern sports, but have a prominent athlete in a starring role.

If a sports film was not included, it was usually for one of two reasons. Either the available posters do not depict a sports scene or no posters whatsoever could be located. Since this is a pictorial overview, I chose those posters that depicted a sports scene over those that did not. I will eventually be publishing a follow-up volume, so if you have posters you would like included, or titles you would like to see, please contact me.

Unless indicated otherwise, the illustrations are of one-sheet posters (41" x 27"). Other sizes included are lobby cards (11" x 14"), half-sheets (22" x 28"), inserts (36" x 14"), three-sheets (81" x 41"), six-sheets (81" x 81"), and foreign posters (varying sizes).

This is not a catalog of posters for sale, nor do I sell reproductions. The posters depicted are from private collections. However, I do sell vintage movie posters of all sorts (through auction and mail order), so if you are interested in acquiring some, or if you want to purchase past or future volumes in this series, please contact me.

- Bruce Hershenson

I Ancient Sports

1 BEN-HUR, 1925, lobby card

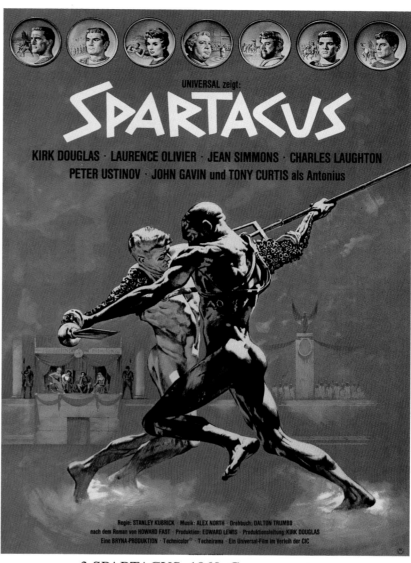

3 SPARTACUS, 1960, German poster

2 BEN-HUR, 1959, lobby card

The images in this book are organized alphabetically by sport, with the images within each sport in (mostly) chronological order. An effort was made to include films from different eras within each sport, but this was not always possible.

II Arm Wrestling

4 P.K. AND THE KID, 1982

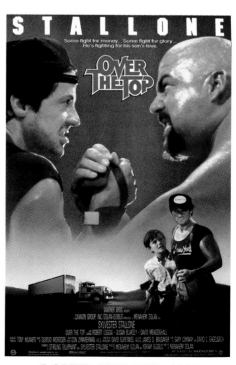

5 OVER THE TOP, 1987

III Auto Racing

6 SPORTING YOUTH, 1924

7 CALIFORNIA OR BUST, 1927, campaign book ad

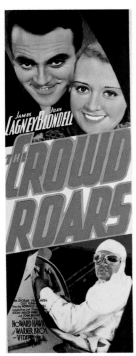

8 THE CROWD ROARS, 1932, insert

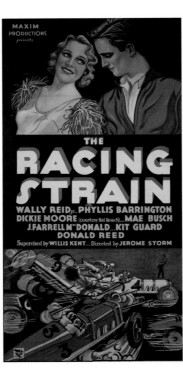

9 THE RACING STRAIN, 1933, three-sheet

10 SPEED DEVILS, 1935

11 RIDE 'EM COWBOY!, 1936, three-sheet

12 INDIANAPOLIS SPEEDWAY, 1939,
"other company" one-sheet

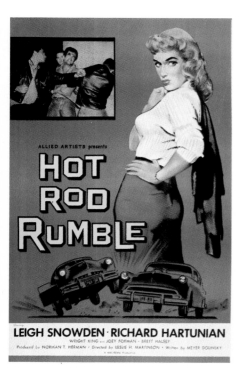

13 HOT ROD RUMBLE, 1957

14 DRAGSTRIP GIRL, 1957

15 SPEED CRAZY, 1959

16 THE WILD RIDE, 1960

17 THE FAST LADY, 1962, British six-sheet

18 GRAND PRIX, 1966

19 WINNING, 1969, lobby card

20 THOSE DARING YOUNG MEN IN
THEIR JAUNTY JALOPIES, 1969

21 LE MANS, 1971

22 THE GUMBALL RALLY, 1976

23 GREASED LIGHTING, 1977

24 CORVETTE SUMMER, 1979

25 SIX PACK, 1982

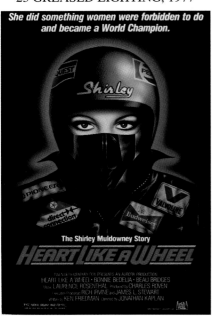

26 HEART LIKE A WHEEL, 1983

27 STROKER ACE, 1983

28 DAYS OF THUNDER, 1990

IV Baseball

29 BREAKING INTO THE BIG
LEAGUE, 1913, trade ad

30 THE PINCH HITTER, 1917

31 THOSE ATHLETIC GIRLS, 1918

32 HEADIN' HOME, 1920, title lobby card

33 HIS NEW MAMMA, 1924

34 THE NEW KLONDIKE, 1926, lobby card

35 SLIDE, KELLY, SLIDE, 1927, herald

36 BABE COMES HOME, 1927

37 BABE COMES HOME, 1927, lobby card

38 CASEY AT THE BAT, 1927

39 WARMING UP, 1928, lobby card

40 CASEY AT THE BAT, 1927, campaign book ad

41 ELMER, THE GREAT, 1933

ACKNOWLEDGEMENTS

After completing the last volume in this series, **Academy Award**® **Winners' Movie Posters**, I contacted **Richard Allen**, who had been instrumental in assembling that book, and also the previous volume, **Cowboy Movie Posters**. I asked him if he had a choice for what the next volume should be. He chose sports films, and was able to provide me with a large number of images that I didn't already have. Originally, Richard wanted this book to have an even wider scope, including all sorts of competitive endeavors, such as fishing, bull-fighting, ballet, cheerleading, and so on, but space limitations required I narrow the focus to more traditional sports. When I eventually do a follow-up volume, I will go back to Richard's original vision.

Since this book was **Richard Allen's** idea, and since he provided many of the images for it, his name appears with mine on the title page. However, the editing and layout were my responsibility, so any errors or deficiencies in this book are mine alone. **Richard Allen** was one of the first proponents of movie posters as a legitimate art form, and he has selflessly devoted more than ten years to rescuing posters and promoting the hobby. Everyone who enjoys looking at these images owes him a huge debt of gratitude.

In order to make this book even more complete, I turned to individuals who have a special interest in sports memorabilia. **Bill Hughes** (co-owner of Executive Gallery in Newport Beach, CA) provided many rare images. Bill sells and auctions movie posters, sports and rock & roll memorabilia, and comic books. **Jerry Zuckerman** (Tary Enterprises, Oradell, NJ) also provided many rare images. Jerry sells all sorts of movie posters, but specializes in sports films. **Konstantine Spanoudis** (Cinema Art Gallery, Fort Lee, NJ) provided three one-of-a-kind three-sheet images. Konstantine sells movie posters of all kinds, especially those with great graphics.

The poster on the cover of this book, **Babe Comes Home**, comes from the collection of **Ira Resnick**. Ira purchased the poster, the only known copy, from a dealer in 1986, for six hundred dollars. If he chose to sell it, it would probably sell for at least a hundred times that price today! Ira owns the **Motion Picture Arts Gallery** in Manhattan, New York, which provided several other images for this book. The Gallery (managed by **Joe Burtis**) has one of the largest inventories of movie posters for sale, both in quantity and quality.

I also contacted several people who had a single poster that I knew would add to the quality of this volume. **Woody Wise** provided his one-sheet poster from **The Game That Kills**, and **Matt Schapiro** provided his original German **Olympia** poster. **Barry Goldman** literally risked life and limb to provide his magnificent title lobby card from **Headin' Home**. **William Hewitt** provided his **Pro Football** one-sheet that appears on the back cover. All of these individuals went to great trouble to provide assistance and I give them my deepest thanks.

I need to thank **John Sawyer** and **John Hazelton**, who indirectly provided images for this volume, as well as previous ones. Both have a great love of movie posters, and have been generous with their help.

When I had most of the material for this volume completed, I contacted **Morrie Everett**, who has helped me with each volume. Morrie has the virtually impossible goal of collecting a poster or lobby card from every film ever made. In thirty years he has acquired examples from nearly 70,000 different titles!

Morrie spent several days combing his collection for images from sports films. He provided many titles, both important ones that had eluded me, and obscure ones, from which he may have the only surviving example. Morrie has spent a huge amount of time and energy on each of my projects and I can't thank him enough. Morrie owns two stores (**The Last Moving Picture Co.** in Hollywood and Cleveland) and co-owns a photo-leasing business (**The Everett Collection** in New York City). Those seeking to buy a poster, lobby card or still of a specific film or star would do well to call them first.

If this book has a better look than most picture books you see, it is because of the talents of those who assembled it. **Sylvia Hershenson** brought together the written material and did the proofreading. Many of the posters were photographed by **David Graveen**. The book was printed by Courier Graphics, under the guidance of **Ginger Dickinson**.

I wish to dedicate this book to Sylvia. Throughout my life, people have told me that I have gotten more lucky breaks than anyone else they know. I always thought that was an exaggeration, but since I married Sylvia, I have become a believer! Thank you, Sylvia, for all you've added to my life.

- Bruce Hershenson
West Plains, Missouri
June 1996

SPORTS MOVIE POSTERS INDEX

NOTES

(Note: Certainly entire books could be written about this subject and many sports could have separate books devoted to them. These notes are intended to provide a few interesting tidbits about several of the genres.)

III Auto Racing: More than a hundred auto racing films have been made. In recent years, this subject has fallen out of favor, probably due in large part to the great expense involved, and the public's growing sophistication regarding the use of stunt doubles. However, new computer techniques may allow for a resurgence of this genre, with more spectacular effects than ever before.

IV Baseball: Baseball movies come in clumps, as do all sports films. Once a successful film is released, most of the other studios release one of their own. There was a period in the late 1960's and early 1970's when virtually no baseball films (or any sports films for that matter) were made. This was probably because sports films tend to have an All-American flavor that was out of step with the anti-war sentiment of the time. The late 1980's and 1990's have seen a resurgence of sports films in general, and baseball films in particular.

Number 32 (Headin' Home) was a film made to showcase the talents of fledgling superstar Babe Ruth in 1920. Ruth was promised the then-staggering sum of $50,000 to appear in the film, but the producers went broke and Ruth was never paid.

VIII Boxing: While there have been hundreds of filmed versions of actual boxing matches, this volume excludes those (with the exception of two, #111 and #114). Instead, this volume covers some of the hundreds of films with a boxing storyline. Fight pictures were extremely popular in the 1920s-1940s, but fell into a severe decline. Rocky, in 1976, single-handedly revived the genre, but it has begun slumping again in recent years.

X Golf: Golf (like bowling, bicycling, tennis, and many other sports) is played by millions, but it is very difficult to build a movie around a sport that is not very dramatic to watch. Films about these sports tend to fall either in the instructional category or in the broad slapstick category, often with cartoon characters taking the pratfalls.

XI Horse Racing: Hundreds of films have been made with a race track setting, as the inherent drama of a horse race (combined with the usual gambling, often with the hero betting everything on a long shot) is a natural theme for the movies. However, race tracks have declined in recent years as other forms of gambling have been legalized, and there has been a precipitous decline in the number of racing films.

XIV Martial Arts: The success in the United States of this genre is due entirely to the remarkable Bruce Lee. Though he made only a handful of films, hundreds were made in the 1970s, and the genre continues to this day, led by Jackie Chan.

XVII Olympic Sports: Several documentaries have been made about different Olympiads, with the most famous being the one directed by Leni Riefenstahl, Olympia, about the 1936 Berlin Olympics. Also, several biographical films have been made about individual Olympic champions.

XXXI Movie Studios Sports Series: In the days before television, newsreels were loaded with sports footage. The studios began releasing individual sports newsreels, each under a different name, many with a "name" announcer.

XXXII Collegiate Films: Virtually every film that takes place at a college has at least one sports sequence, and often the entire film is centered on athletic competition. A handful of the hundreds of such films are presented here.

XXXIII Non-Sports Films Featuring Sports Stars: A huge number of star athletes have taken a stab at acting, usually with depressing results. Not surprisingly, many come from boxing and football, where careers are often spectacular, but short in duration.

XXXIV Sports of the Future: A few films have attempted to predict new sports that will emerge in the 21st century, and they have always been ultra-violent. Thankfully, this trend has not been coming to pass, as measures are being taken to reduce the violence in the sports that already exist.

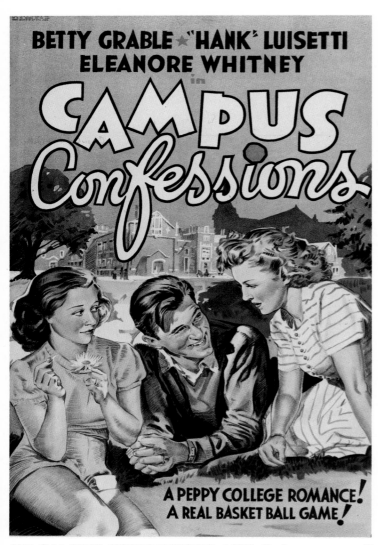

377 CAMPUS CONFESSIONS, 1938, "other company"
one-sheet

378 HERCULES, 1983

XXXIV Sports of the Future

379 ROLLERBALL, 1975

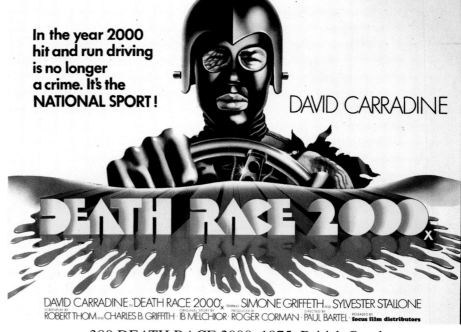

380 DEATH RACE 2000, 1975, British Quad

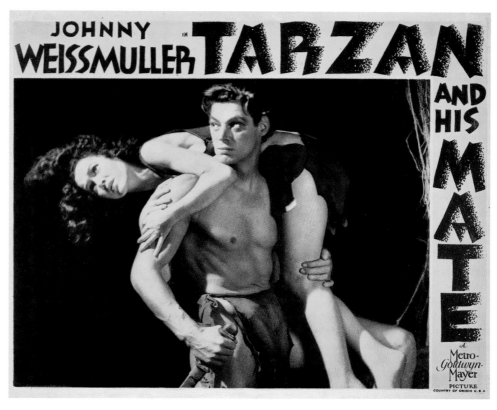

373 TARZAN AND HIS MATE, 1934, lobby card

Rarely have sports stars achieved such success in films that their sports accomplishments have been largely forgotten. Both Johnny Weissmuller and Buster Crabbe were Olympic Gold medalists in swimming prior to their long, illustrious film careers.

372 TARZAN THE APE MAN, 1932, Australian daybill

374 HOLD'EM YALE, 1935

375 SOUL SOLDIER, 1972

376 FIESTA, 1947

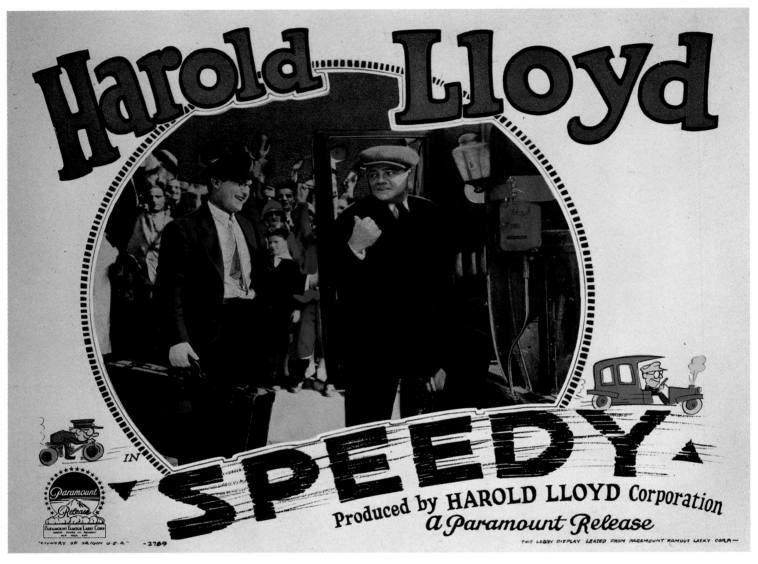

368 SPEEDY, 1928, lobby card

369 RAWHIDE, 1938

370 MANHATTAN
MERRY-GO-ROUND, 1937

371 GERONIMO!, 1962

363 KING OF THE TEXAS RANGERS, 1941

364 THE THING WITH TWO HEADS, 1972

365 THE GLOVE, 1980

366 THE HARD HEADS, 1980

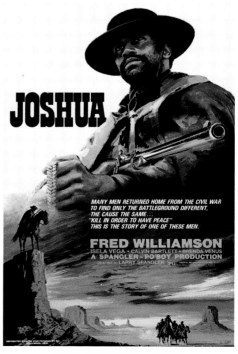

367 JOSHUA, 1976

359 100 RIFLES, 1969

In the late 1960s, the growing civil rights and black power movements led to an onslaught of films created by black filmmakers and starring largely all-black casts. This subject deserves an entire book of its own, and a future volume in this series will be devoted to it.

Two great football players, Jim Brown and Fred Williamson, quit football to become full-time film stars, and the volume of their work has been truly impressive.

360 TAKE A HARD RIDE, 1975

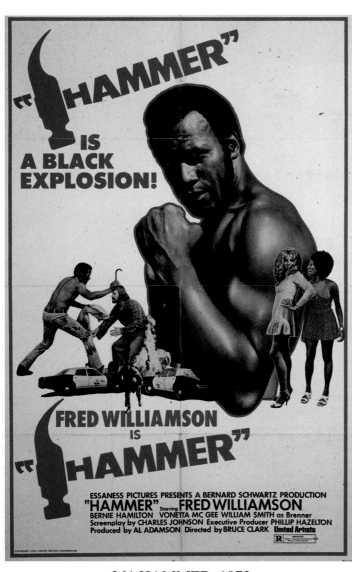

361 HAMMER, 1972

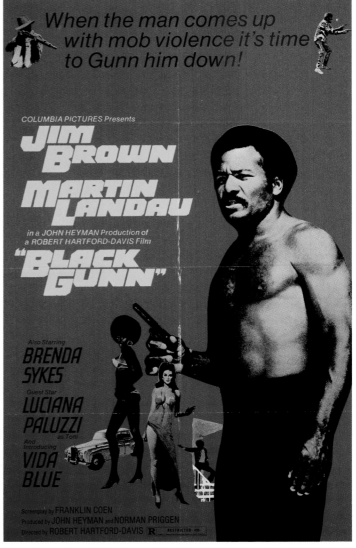

362 BLACK GUNN, 1972

XXXIII Non-Sports Films Featuring Sports Stars

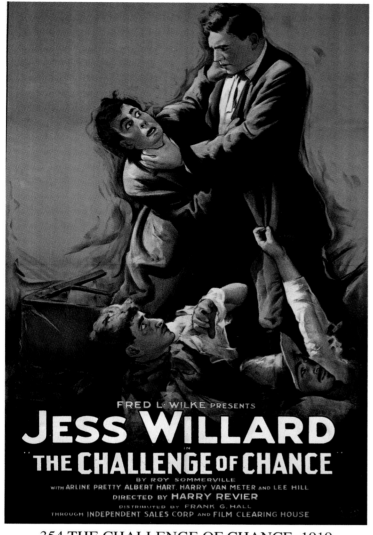

354 THE CHALLENGE OF CHANCE, 1919

355 THE MIDNIGHT MAN, 1919,
three-sheet

356 THE FIGHTING MARINE,
1926

357 MANDOM, MOD OCH SKONA
KVINNOR, circa 1933, Swedish poster
for German film

358 THE PITTSBURGH KID,
1941

XXXII Collegiate Films

349 COLLEGE, 1927

350 SO THIS IS COLLEGE, 1929

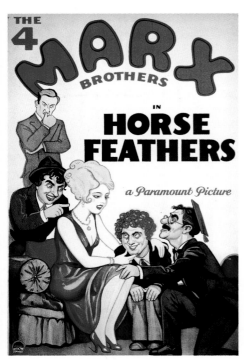

351 HORSE FEATHERS, 1932

352 COLLEGE SWING,
1938, three-sheet

353 HOLD THAT CO-ED, 1938,
six-sheet

XXXI Movie Studio Sports Series

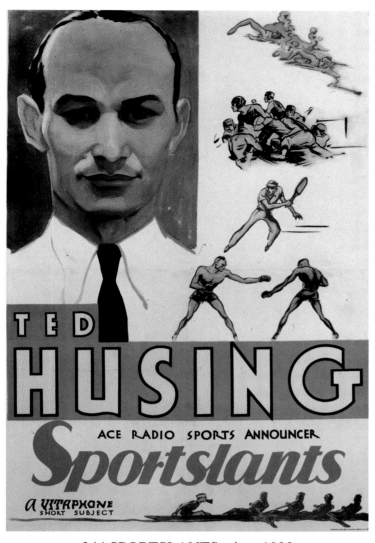

344 SPORTSLANTS, circa 1933

345 ED THORGERSEN'S SPORTS REVIEWS,
circa 1939

346 SPORT CHAMPIONS,
circa 1931

347 SPORTSCOPE, circa 1938

348 WORLD OF SPORTS,
circa 1933

339 THE GLADIATOR, 1938

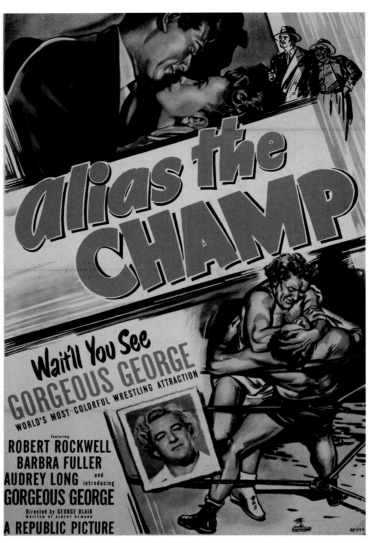

340 ALIAS THE CHAMP, 1949

341 ALIAS THE CHAMP,
1949, three-sheet

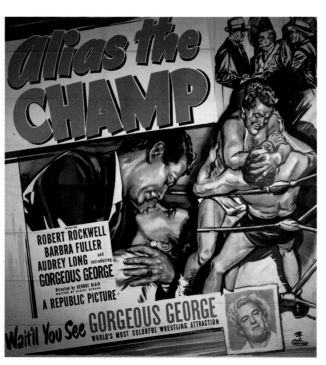

342 ALIAS THE CHAMP, 1949, six-sheet

343 THE ONE AND ONLY,
1978

324 WATER JAMBOREE, 1932

325 BATHING BEAUTY, 1944

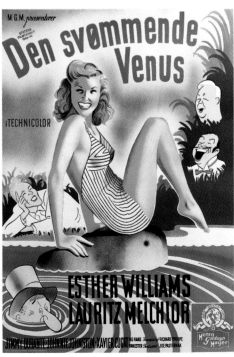

326 BATHING BEAUTY, 1944

327 THIS TIME FOR KEEPS,
1947, Danish poster

328 LIFEGUARD, 1976

320 FOLLOW ME, 1966, lobby card

321 NORTH SHORE, 1987

322 PACIFIC VIBRATIONS, 1971

323 THE ENDLESS SUMMER II, 1994

305 THE FIREBALL, 1950

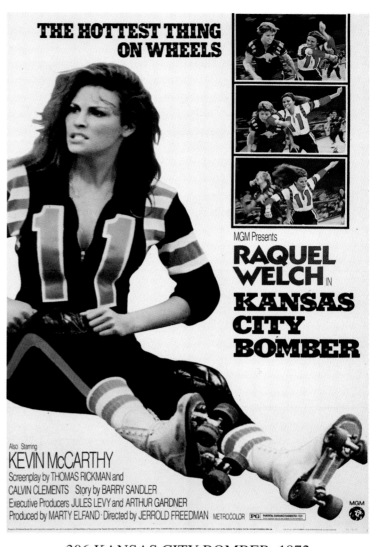

306 KANSAS CITY BOMBER, 1972

307 SKATETOWN USA, 1979

308 GLEAMING THE CUBE, 1988

309 AIRBORNE, 1993

300 THE BULL-DOGGER, 1923, three-sheet

301 THE CALGARY STAMPEDE, 1925

302 LET 'ER BUCK, 1925

303 BLACK RODEO, 1972

304 8 SECONDS, 1994

XX Rafting

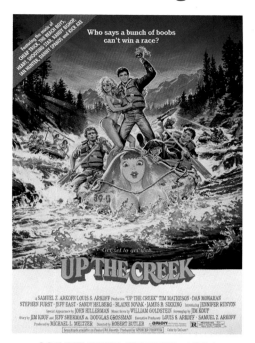

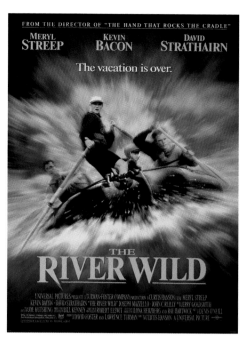

295 UP THE CREEK, 1984

296 THE RIVER WILD, 1994, advance one-sheet

297 THE RIVER WILD, 1994

XXI Rowing

298 FOREVER AFTER, 1926, campaign book ad

299 ROW ROW ROW, 1928/29, campaign book ad

Few films have been made concerning pool (pocket billiards). One of these, **The Hustler**, was a success on all levels. It had some of the finest stars of the day, and was expertly written and directed. It not only captured the world of professional pool players, but also masterfully delved into the psychology of all professional and compulsive gamblers.

290 THIS SPORTING AGE, 1931

291 POLO JOE, 1936

XIX Pool

292 THE HUSTLER, 1961, lobby card

293 THE HUSTLER, 1961, lobby card

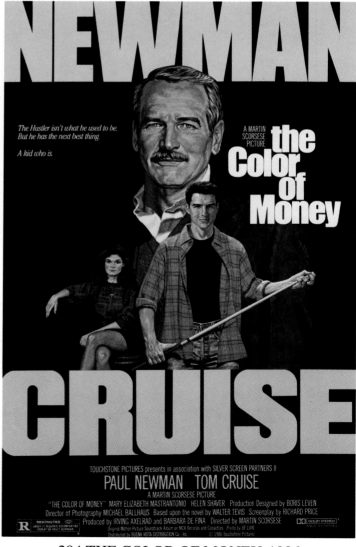

294 THE COLOR OF MONEY, 1986

286 JIM THORPE-ALL AMERICAN, 1951, lobby card

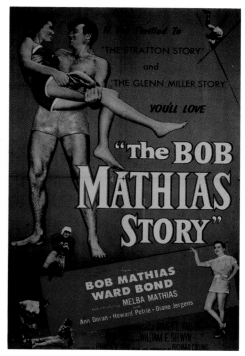

287 THE BOB MATHIAS STORY, 1954

288 CHARIOTS OF FIRE, 1981

289 GYMKATA, 1985

281 OLYMPIA, 1938, German poster

282 XIVth OLYMPIAD THE GLORY OF SPORT, 1948, English poster

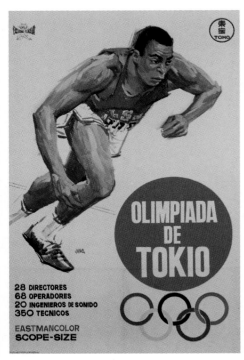

283 TOKYO OLYMPIAD, 1966, Spanish poster for Japanese film

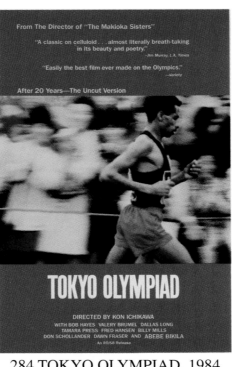

284 TOKYO OLYMPIAD, 1984 reissue of 1966 film

285 THE GAMES, 1967

XVI Mountain Climbing

276 IM KAMPF MIT DEM BERGE, circa 1915,
Swedish poster

277 LAVINEN, circa 1930,
Swedish poster for German film

278 FIVE DAYS ONE SUMMER,
1982

279 K2 THE ULTIMATE HIGH,
1992

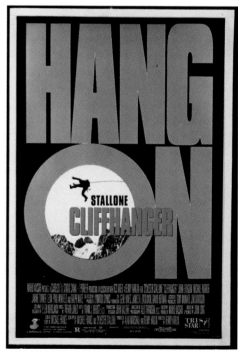

280 CLIFFHANGER, 1993

XV Motorcycling

271 ON ANY SUNDAY, 1971

272 ON ANY SUNDAY, 1971

273 EVEL KNIEVEL, 1971

274 VIVA KNIEVEL, 1977

275 FAST CHARLIE, 1979

255 ONE IN A MILLION, 1936, Swedish poster

256 THE ICE FOLLIES OF 1939, 1939

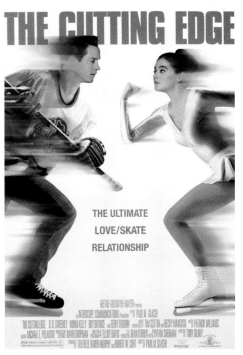

257 ICE-CAPADES, 1941

258 SILVER SKATES, 1942

259 THE CUTTING EDGE, 1992

251 RIDE KELLY RIDE, 1941

252 NATIONAL VELVET, 1945, lobby card

253 INTERNATIONAL VELVET, 1978

254 PHAR LAP, 1983

246 KENTUCKY BLUE STREAK, 1935

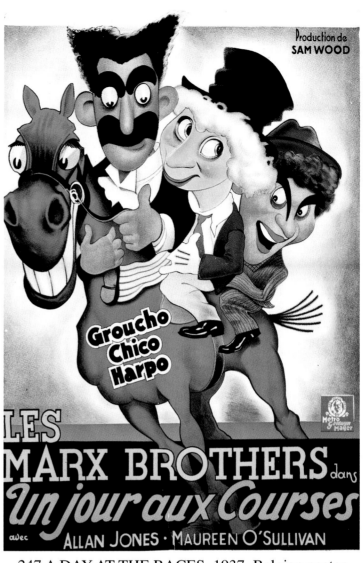

247 A DAY AT THE RACES, 1937, Belgian poster

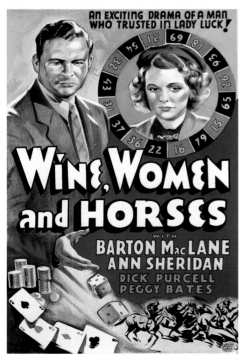

248 WINE, WOMEN AND HORSES, 1937, "other company" one-sheet

249 STRAIGHT PLACE AND SHOW, 1938, three-sheet

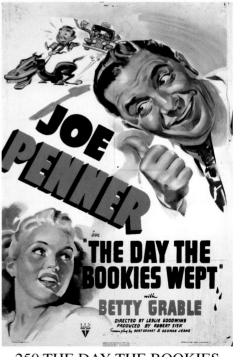

250 THE DAY THE BOOKIES WEPT, 1939

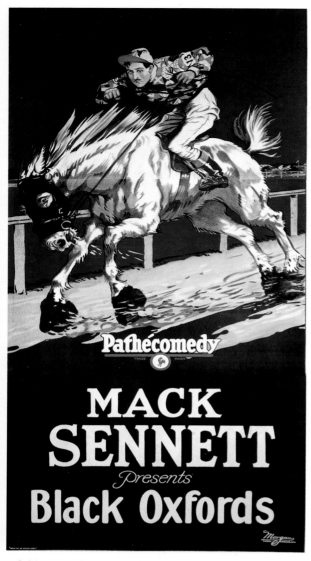

241 BLACK OXFORDS, 1924, three-sheet

242 THE DUKE OF LADIES,1926/27, campaign book ad

243 MISS JOCKEY, 1927,
campaign book ad

244 SPORTING BLOOD, 1931,
Swedish poster

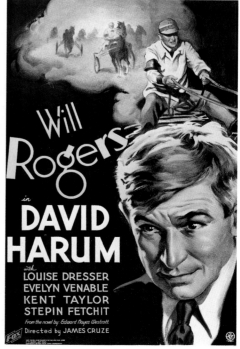

245 DAVID HARUM, 1934

237 ATTA BOY'S LAST RACE,
1916, three-sheet

238 WINNING THE FUTURITY, 1926, title lobby card

239 DERBY DAY, 1923

240 THE FLAMING CRISIS, 1924

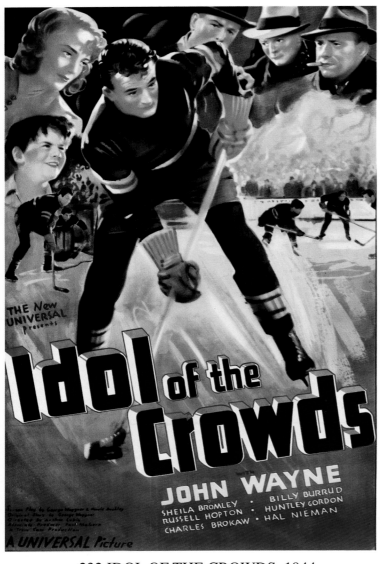

232 IDOL OF THE CROWDS, 1944

233 WHITE LIGHTNING, 1953

234 SLAP SHOT, 1977

235 THE MIGHTY DUCKS, 1992

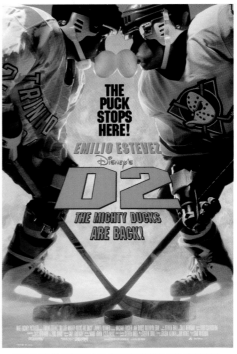

236 D2 THE MIGHTY DUCKS
ARE BACK!, 1994

204 TWO MINUTE WARNING, 1976

205 BLACK SUNDAY, 1977

206 SEMI-TOUGH, 1977

207 SEMI-TOUGH, 1977

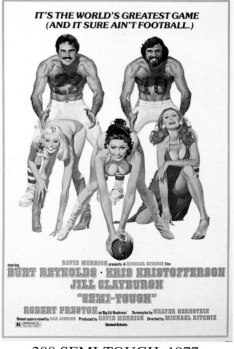

208 SEMI-TOUGH, 1977

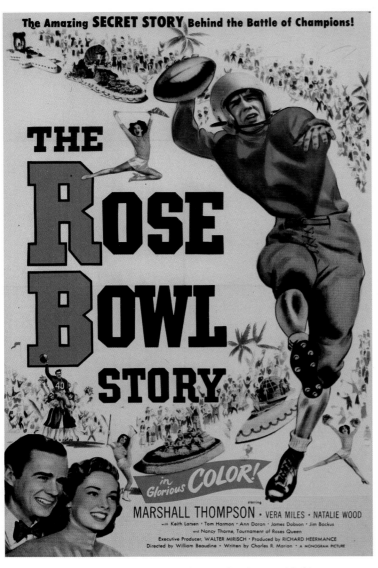

200 THE ROSE BOWL STORY, 1952

201 CRAZYLEGS, 1953

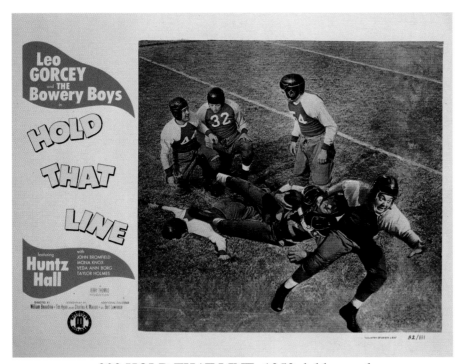

202 HOLD THAT LINE, 1952, lobby card

203 PAPER LION, 1968

195 KNUTE ROCKNE ALL
AMERICAN, 1940

196 WHILE THOUSANDS CHEER, 1940

197 KNUTE ROCKNE ALL
AMERICAN, 1940, three-sheet

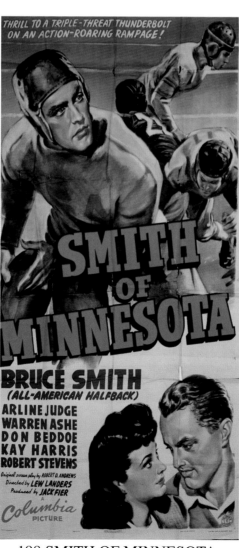

198 SMITH OF MINNESOTA,
1942, three-sheet

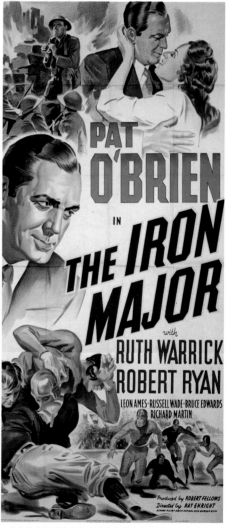

199 THE IRON MAJOR, 1943,
three-sheet

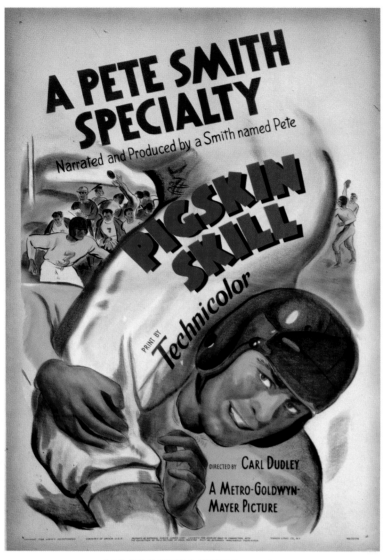

190 PIGSKIN SKILL, 1937

191 TWO MINUTES TO PLAY, 1937,
three-sheet

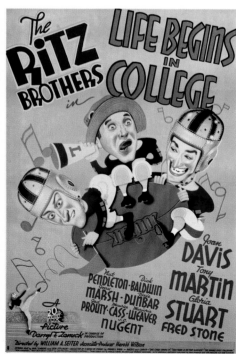

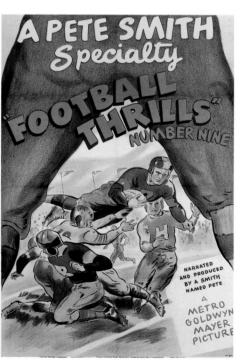

192 LIFE BEGINS IN COLLEGE,
1937

193 FOOTBALL THRILLS
(NUMBER 9), 1938

194 THE COWBOY QUARTERBACK,
1939, "other company" one-sheet

185 THAT'S MY BOY, 1932

186 ALL AMERICAN, 1932,
campaign book ad

187 RACKETY RAX, 1932

188 ROSE BOWL, 1936

189 THE BIG GAME, 1936

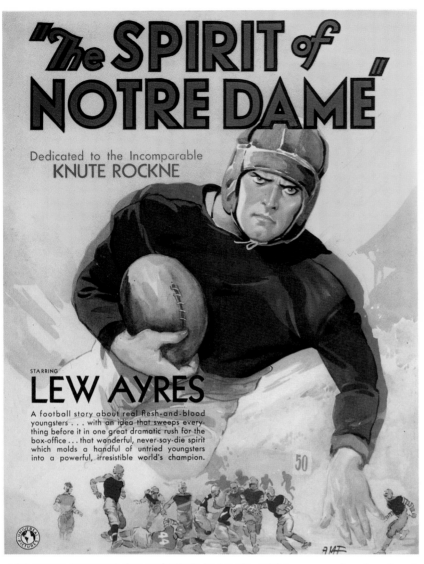

180 THE SPIRIT OF NOTRE DAME, 1931, campaign book ad

181 THE SPIRIT OF NOTRE DAME, 1931

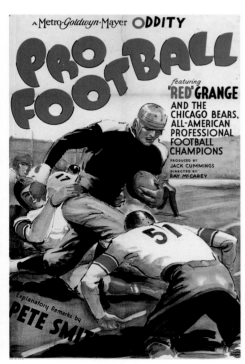

182 PRO FOOTBALL, 1931

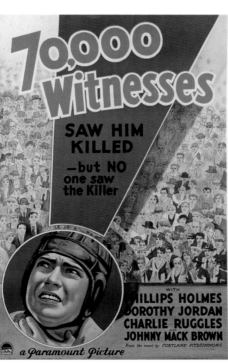

183 70,000 WITNESSES, 1932

184 HOLD 'EM JAIL, 1932

175 BROWN OF HARVARD, 1926

176 BROWN OF HARVARD, 1926, window card

177 WIN THAT GIRL, 1928, campaign book ad

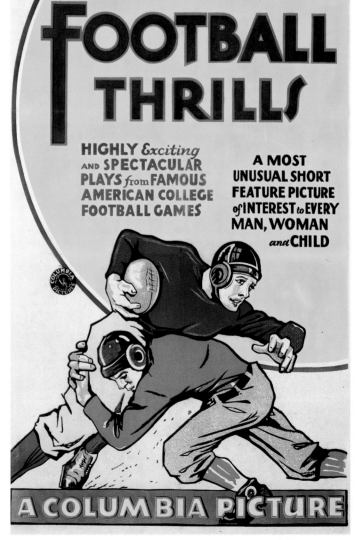

178 MICKEY'S STAMPEDE, 1931

179 FOOTBALL THRILLS, 1931

IX Football

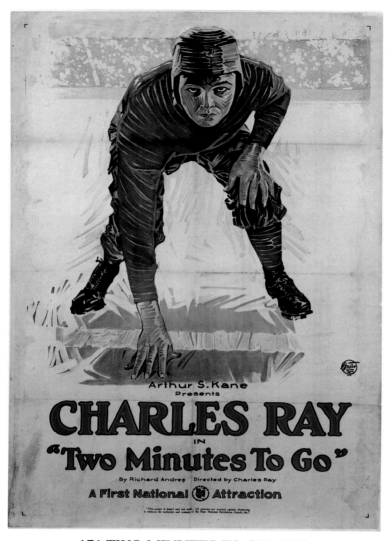

171 TWO MINUTES TO GO, 1921

172 FEET OF MUD, 1924, three-sheet

173 THE QUARTERBACK, 1926,
campaign book ad

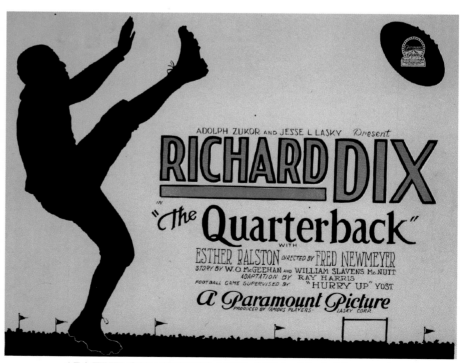

174 THE QUARTERBACK, 1926, title lobby card

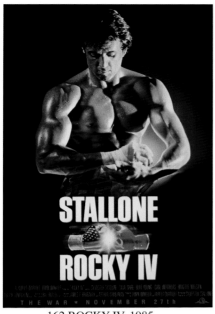

162 ROCKY IV, 1985

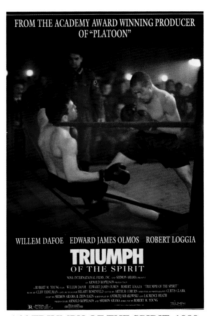

163 ROCKY IV, 1985

164 NO RETREAT NO SURRENDER, 1986

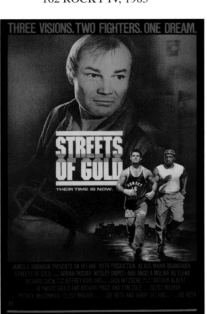

165 STREETS OF GOLD, 1986

166 TRIUMPH OF THE SPIRIT, 1989

167 ROCKY V, 1990

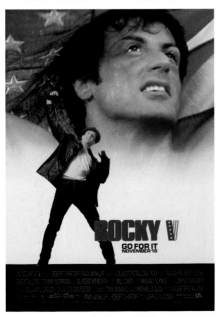

168 ROCKY V, 1990

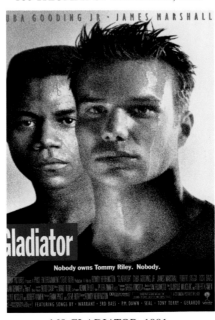

169 GLADIATOR, 1991

170 DIGGSTOWN, 1992

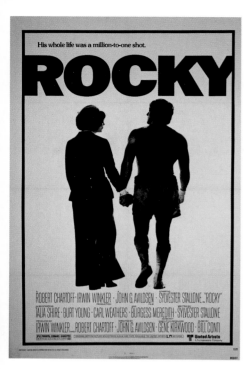

157 ROCKY, 1976

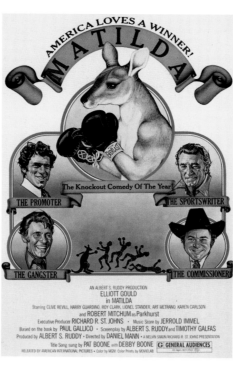

158 MATILDA, 1978

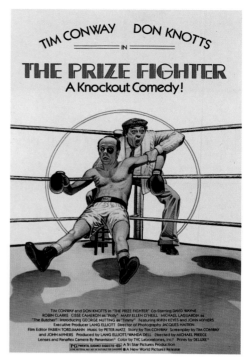

159 THE PRIZE FIGHTER, 1979

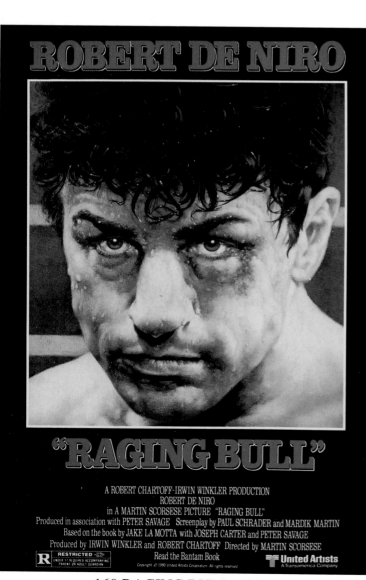

160 RAGING BULL, 1980

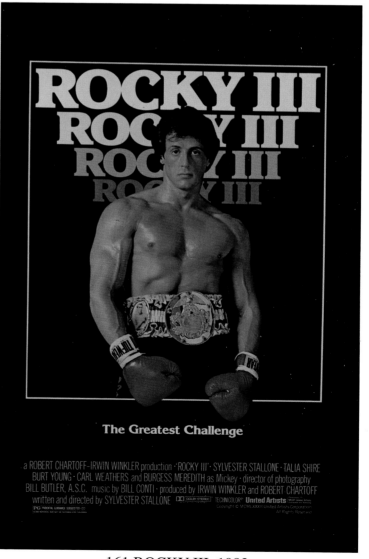

161 ROCKY III, 1982

154 THE HARDER THEY FALL, 1956,
pressbook cover

155 A.K.A. CASSIUS CLAY, 1970,
half sheet

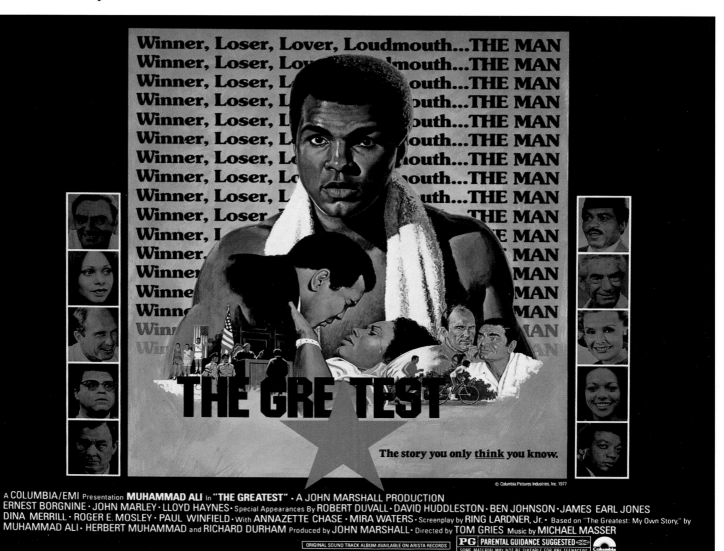

156 THE GREATEST, 1977, half-sheet

150 THE GOLDEN GLOVES STORY, 1950

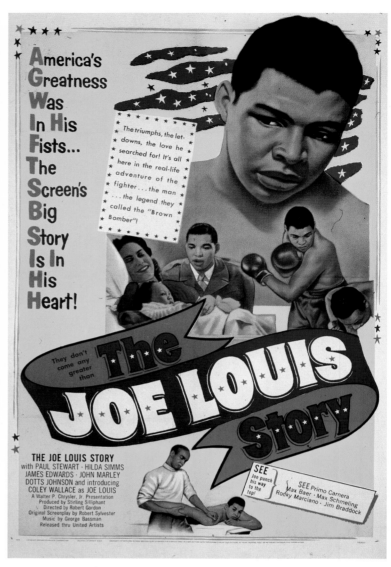

151 THE JOE LOUIS STORY, 1953

152 FROM HERE TO ETERNITY, 1953, lobby card

153 SOMEBODY UP THERE
LIKES ME, 1956

146 BODY AND SOUL, 1947, title lobby card

147 THE FIGHT NEVER ENDS, 1947

148 IN THIS CORNER, 1948

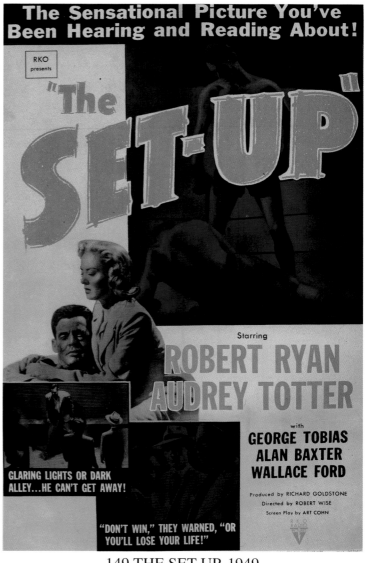

149 THE SET-UP, 1949

142 CITY FOR CONQUEST, 1939, lobby card

143 THEY MADE ME A
CRIMINAL, 1939

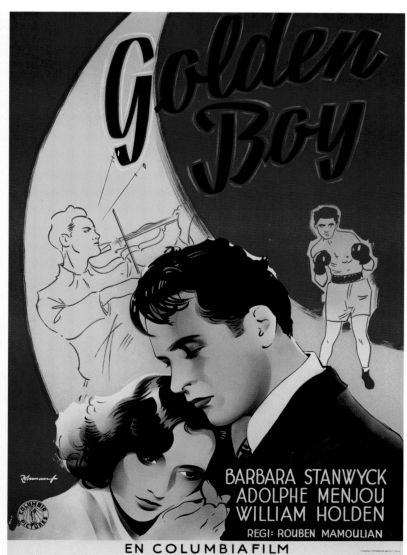

144 GOLDEN BOY, 1939, Swedish poster

145 JOE PALOOKA CHAMPION, 1946,
Belgian poster

137 FOR THE LOVE OF PETE, 1936

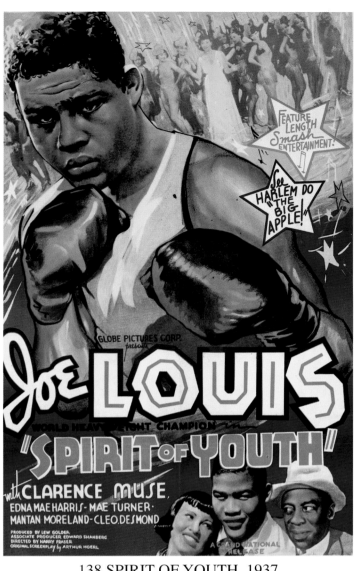

138 SPIRIT OF YOUTH, 1937

139 THE KID COMES BACK,
1937, "other company" one-sheet

140 TAKING THE COUNT, 1937

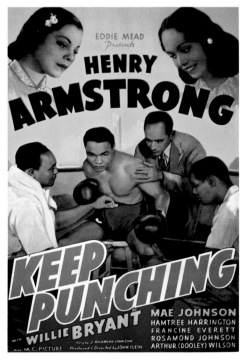

141 KEEP PUNCHING, 1939

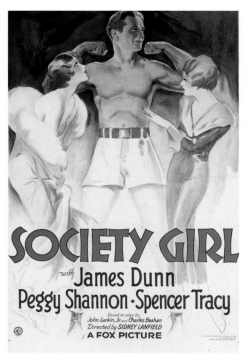

131 SOCIETY GIRL, 1932

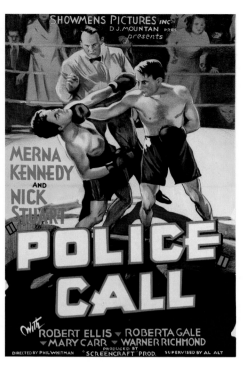

132 POLICE CALL, 1933

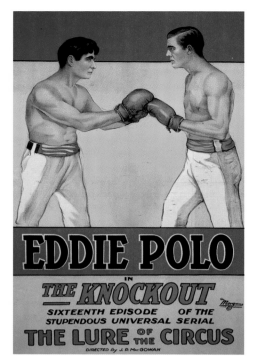

133 THE KNOCKOUT, 1935

134 CAIN AND MABEL, 1936, title lobby card

135 CAIN AND MABEL, 1936, lobby card

136 KELLY THE SECOND, 1936

125 THE BIG FIGHT, 1930

126 HOLD EVERYTHING, 1930

127 THE CHAMP, 1931

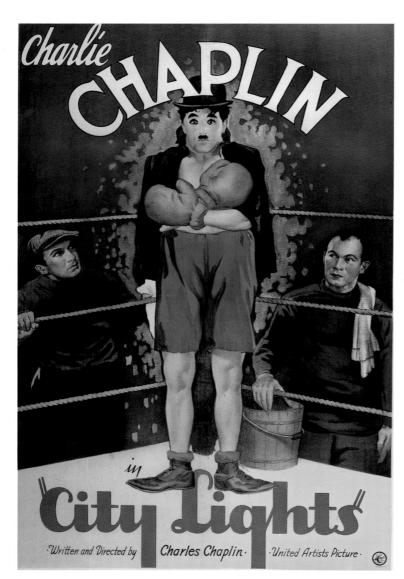

128 CITY LIGHTS, 1931

129 THE CHAMP, 1931, lobby card

130 WINNER TAKE ALL, 1932, lobby card

120 THE DANGEROUS COWARD, 1924

121 BATTLING BUTLER,
1926, insert

122 THE RING, 1927,
Australian daybill

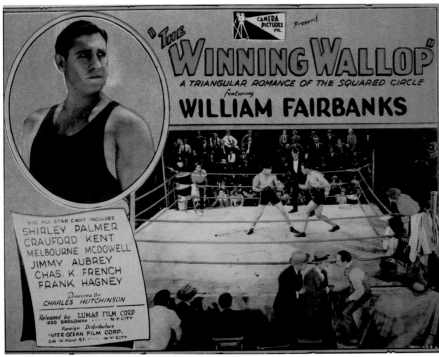

123 THE WINNING WALLOP, 1926, title lobby card

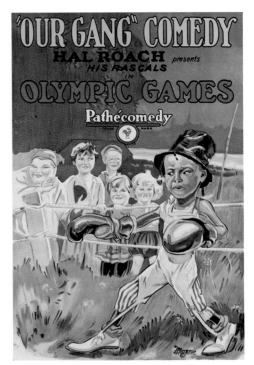

124 OLYMPIC GAMES, 1927

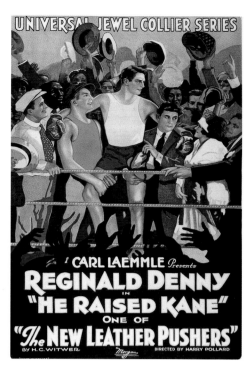

116 THE LEATHER PUSHERS
ROUND ONE, 1922

117 THE WANDERING TWO,
1923

118 HE RAISED KANE, 1923

119 THE CHICKASHA BONE CRUSHER, 1923, title lobby card

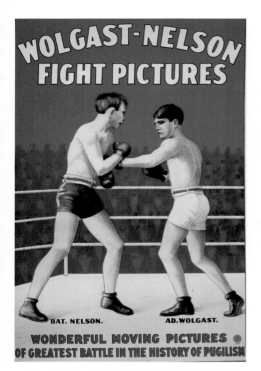

111 WOLGAST-NELSON FIGHT PICTURES, 1908

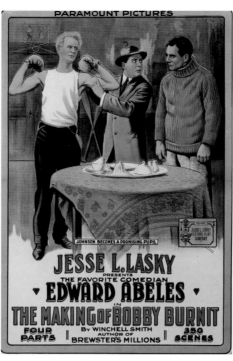

112 THE MAKING OF BOBBY BURNIT, 1914

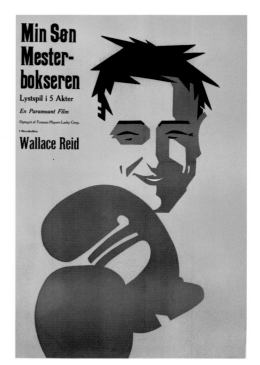

113 THE WORLD'S CHAMPION, 1923, Danish poster

VIII Boxing

Boxing was an enormously popular sport in the 1910s and 1920s, and a huge number of fictional films with a boxing theme were made. In addition, actual fights were filmed, and beautiful stone lithographed posters were made to promote the movies. Sadly, almost none of these are known to have survived. The most popular silent boxing films were those in **The Leather Pushers** series, of which several dozen were made.

114 JACK DEMPSEY AND GEORGES CARPENTIER, 1921

115 ALL'S SWELL ON THE OCEAN, 1922, lobby card

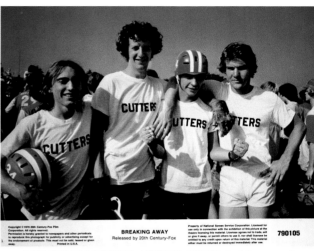

107 BREAKING AWAY, 1979, lobby card

106 6 DAY BIKE RIDER, 1934

While bicycling and bowling are two of the most popular participatory sports, the basic repetitiveness of both sports make for very uninteresting films, unless they are of an instructional or comedic nature.

108 STRIKES AND SPARES, 1934

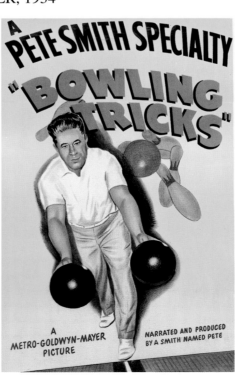

109 BOWLING TRICKS, 1948

110 DREAMER, 1979

97 INSIDE MOVES, 1980

98 THAT CHAMPIONSHIP SEASON, 1982

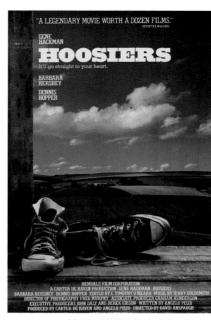

99 HOOSIERS, 1986

100 HEAVEN IS A PLAYGROUND, 1991

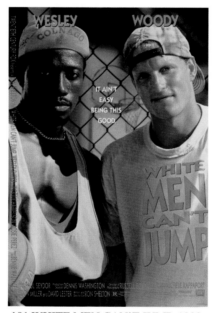

101 WHITE MEN CAN'T JUMP, 1992

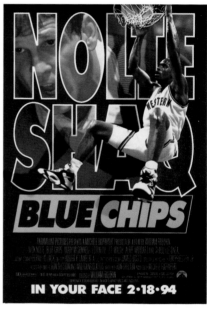

102 BLUE CHIPS, 1994

103 ABOVE THE RIM, 1994

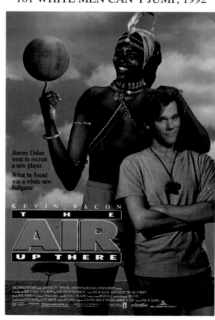

104 THE AIR UP THERE, 1994

105 HOOP DREAMS, 1995

93 CORNBREAD EARL AND ME, 1975

94 ONE FLEW OVER THE CUCKOO'S NEST, 1975

95 THE FISH THAT SAVED PITTSBURGH, 1978

96 THE GREAT SANTINI, 1979

89 THE HARLEM GLOBE-TROTTERS,1952

90 THE HARLEM GLOBE-TROTTERS,1952,
British Quad

V Basketball

Few films were made about basketball before the 1970s, with the main exception being two films about the legendary Harlem Globe-Trotters. The sports' surge in popularity in the 1980s and 1990s has resulted in a large number of films, a trend that is sure to continue.

91 GO, MAN, GO!, 1954

92 GO, MAN, GO!, 1954, half-sheet